THE ORIGINAL SLOW COOKER COOKBOOK #2021

Delicious and Quick Recipes for the Whole Family incl. Special Slow Cooker Desserts

BETHANY GORDON

ISBN - 9798698058427

TABLE OF CONTENTS

Welcome to 'The Original Slow Cooker Book #2021'!

Enjoy experimenting with over 40 different and exciting recipes, covering breakfast, lunch, dinner, *and* an extra dessert special. Packed with nutritious, delicious, culinary delights for all cooking abilities, this book will welcome you to slow cooking and all the possibilities that come with this nifty machine.

Learn how a slow cooker works, how to care for your machine, and lots of handy tips and tricks to get the most out of your slow cooker.

From beef stew to cookies and cream fudge, from Ireland to Morocco and beyond, take your tastebuds around the world with this exploration of slow cooker opportunities.

So, go and grab a plate and get your slow cooker prepared- it's about to face a lot of use!

PLEASE NOTE ALL RECIPES CONTAINED WITHIN THIS BOOK ARE FOR A 5 LITRE SLOW COOKER

WHAT IS A SLOW COOKER AND HOW DOES IT WORK

First things first: a slow cooker is a machine used for cooking.

A slow cooker is made up of three main parts:

The base	handles and temperature controls
The inner bowl	cooking vessel made of easily heated, insulated material
The lid	to trap in steam and seal in heat

The base controls the heating and temperature regulation in order to cook the food within the bowl at a relatively low, but consistent heat. Slow cookers tend to have 2 temperature setting - a high and low- but some newer models also possess a medium setting, alongside other features to cover different cooking processes. On a traditional slow cooker the high temperature is around 100C // 212F, and the low temperature sits at around 94C // 200F.

Slow cookers are an effective method of cooking. The heat generated in the base rises and insulates the bowl, trapping in heat and facilitating even cooking of your dish. This way of cooking is very similar to a Dutch oven or cooking on a stove, but the technical elements of a slow cooker mean you can safely leave it on without constant supervision.

THE BENEFITS OF USING A SLOW COOKER

- Most slow cookers have an inbuilt timer. This means you can minimally prepare your ingredients, pop them in your slow cooker, and go about your day stress free. A slow cooker is safe to be left unattended, allowing you to come home to a home-cooked meal hassle free.

- Slow cookers are particularly useful for cooking tougher, often cheaper, cuts of meat, because the low, steady heat and trapped moisture are effective in tenderising the meat.

- Slow cookers are cost efficient- alongside being useful for cheaper cuts of meat they are cheaper to run than an oven, and the ease of use can serve as a deterrent against buying takeout's or ready meals.

- A perk of long and low cooking is that is enhances flavour of foods. More complex flavour profiles have time to develop, and a more intense infusion process is possible.

- The process of slow cooking on a low heat means that the nutrients within food remain intact. High heat can degrade nutrients within food, but slow cooking maintains nutrients and prevents dangerous chemicals forming.

- For the novice chef slow cookers are great because it's almost impossible to burn, scorch, or overcook food- the longer it cooks the more moist, tender, and flavoursome the dish becomes!

- Because so many slow cooker dishes are 'one-pot' recipes much less washing up is needed. Slow cookers free up valuable time for parents, professionals, or anyone with a lot on their (metaphorical) plate.

HOW TO CARE FOR A SLOW COOKER

As with anything in life, the more you care for your slow cooker the longer it will last you. Just like any cooking equipment your slow cooker base and bowl need to be cleaned after each use. Do no scour the bowl of your slow cooker, or use abrasive cleaning liquids, as this will degrade the bowl of your slow cooker. Similarly, placing the hot bowl in cold water will easily damage your slow cooker bowl. A slow cooker is electric, so keep the base away from water and be careful with plug sockets for your own personal safety.

TIPS AND TRICKS FOR SLOW COOKING

Don't add oil and trim an excess fat when slow cooking

Fat tends to reduce easily when cooked at a high heat, but this isn't the case with slow cooking, so remove any excess fat for a tastier (and healthier) dish.

Use less liquid with your slow cooker

Liquid that would evaporate with traditional cooking will be trapped in your slow cooker, so be cautious and use less rather than more, especially when adapting recipes.

Don't overfill your slow cooker

This is because of liquid once again- if your slow cooker is overfilled your dish will be ruined and liquid will start to leak beneath the lid.

Use a dishcloth to absorb excess moisture when baking

Place a clean dishcloth over your baking pan (providing the dish won't rise into it) in order to soak up the excess moisture.

Add flour, cornflour, or an alternative thickening agent to sauces

Because liquid doesn't escape sauces won't thicken in a slow cooker. Avoid this problem by adding flour or cornflour to your sauce or draining it and heating it on the stove prior to serving.

Use the 'low' setting as much as possible

When possible always cook your food for longer on a lower temperature. This allows flavour to really develop and is key for the most tender meat.

Don't over season your food

The low and slow cooking allows flavours to develop more intensely and with greater depth, so less seasoning and spices are needed to flavour dishes. Use less rather than more to avoid overpowering your dish's taste.

Leave the lid on as much as possible

Slow cookers are designed to cook without intervention. Constantly checking dishes and removing the lid will also lower the temperature, therefore increasing cooking time. It can be useful to remove steam every once in a while, but doing this too frequently will counteract one of slow cooking's greatest benefits. Each time the lid is lifted another 15 minutes should be added to the cooking time.

Place vegetables at the bottom

Heat rises from the base in a slow cooker, so always have your vegetable nearest the base because they take the longest time to cook. Place meat on top of the vegetables before pouring in your liquid element.

Add pastas, dairy, and soft vegetables later

Add in grains near the end of your cooking time to avoid them absorbing too much liquid and becoming too soft and mushy.

Add in dairy products, especially milk and cream, in the last hour to avoid the mixture from curdling.

Add in soft vegetables in the last hour of cooking to avoid them becoming too soft and mushy.

CONVENTIONAL RECIPE CONVERSIONS

When making a conventional recipe slow cooker appropriate the most important things to consider are **time** and **liquid volume**.

CONVENTIONAL TIME	LOW SETTING	HIGH SETTING
15 – 30 minutes	4 – 6 hours	1 – 2 hours
30 minutes – 1 hour	5 – 7 hours	2 – 3 hours
1 – 2 hours	6 – 8 hours	3 – 4 hours

Etc.

Reduce liquid by 1/3 of overall volume

BREAKFAST

BREAKFAST

Traditionally loved breakfasts: the slow cooker edition! Easily adaptable recipes of firm favourites, all of which can be made overnight for your peace of mind

CHOCOLATE AND BANANA BREAD

SERVES	8
CALORIES	194
CARBOHYDRATES	30.6g
PROTEIN	5.8g
FAT	6.2g

INGREDIENTS

- 100g // 1 c oats
- 250ml // 1 c water
- 1 tsp vanilla bean paste
- 1 tbsp ground cinnamon
- 1 tsp ground nutmeg
- ½ tsp bicarbonate of soda
- 4 medium eggs
- 3 large bananas, overripe
- 2 tbsp honey
- 80g // ½ c dark chocolate chips

DIRECTIONS

1. Start by lining a 8x4 inch loaf pan with parchment paper, leaving the paper long enough to hang over the sides of the pan.

2. Place your oats into a food processor and pulse to form an oat 'flour'. Transfer to a medium mixing bowl and add your water, vanilla bean paste, cinnamon, nutmeg, bicarbonate of soda, and eggs. Beat using a handheld whisk until everything combined to form a smooth batter.

3. In a separate bowl mash your bananas using a fork. Drizzle over your honey and use the fork to mix together. Pour your mashed banana into the batter and beat with your handheld whisk once again. When the banana is fully combined pour the batter into your prepared pan.

4. Sprinkle over the chocolate chips and swirl through a skewer to roughly distribute the chocolate. Place your tin into your slow cooker before setting it to 'high' and leaving to bake for 2-3 hours. Times will vary depending upon your slow cooker, so check every 15-30 minutes once the cake has been baking for 2 hours - this will also release some excess steam that may otherwise affect your cake.

5. Once the cake is baked through and an inserted skewer comes out clean remove it from your slow cooker. Set aside to cool for 10-15 minutes before removing from the pan and slicing. Serve immediately accompanied by strawberry jam and fresh bananas.

BANANA AND CASHEW FRENCH TOAST

SERVES	8
CALORIES	478
CARBOHYDRATES	64.6g
PROTEIN	13.6g
FAT	18.9g

INGREDIENTS

- 1 loaf of stale bread, sliced 1-2 cm thick

- 120g // 4 oz. cream cheese, softened

- 2 medium bananas

- 4 medium eggs

- 250ml // 1 c full fat milk

- 5 tbsp light brown sugar

- 1 tsp vanilla bean paste

- 1 tsp ground cinnamon

- ½ tsp ground nutmeg

- ½ tsp ground ginger

- 2 tbsp salted butter, chilled and grated

- 3 tbsp cashew butter

- 3 tbsp cashew nuts, crushed

DIRECTIONS

1. Spread both sides of your sliced bread with cream cheese and arrange in your slow cooker bowl. In a separate bowl mash your bananas and whisk in your eggs, milk, sugar, vanilla bean paste, cinnamon, nutmeg, and ginger.

2. Pour your milk mixture over your bread and set your low cooker to 'high'. Bake for 2-3 hours, or until the egg has been absorbed by the bread and is cooked, golden, and crisp.

3. Once your French toast has baked turn off the heat and remove the lid from your slow cooker. Sprinkle over your butter and crushed cashew nuts, then drizzle over your cashew butter. Replace the lid and allow your butter to melt.

4. Once your butter has melted serve immediately, accompanied by sliced banana or banana chips.

SAVOURY BACON PORRIDGE

SERVES	8
CALORIES	240
CARBOHYDRATES	20.7g
PROTEIN	16.9g
FAT	10.7g

INGREDIENTS

- 125g // 1 ¼ c oats
- 1 medium sweet potato, peeled and diced
- 1 tbsp salted butter
- 1 garlic clove, minced
- 1 tsp freshly ground black pepper
- 6 cherry tomatoes, quartered
- 6 tbsp grated parmesan
- 1 tsp smoked paprika
- 180ml // ¾ c vegetable stock
- 500ml // 2 c milk
- water as needed
- 8 bacon rashers

DIRECTIONS

1. Place your oats, sweet potato, butter, garlic, pepper, tomatoes, parmesan, paprika, vegetable stock, and milk into the bowl of your slow cooker. Stir to roughly combine, then set your slow cooker to 'high' and leave to cook for 3 hours, stirring every 30 minutes to ensure even cooking time. If your oats get too thick add water as is necessary.

2. Once the oats are cooked turn off the heat but leave them as they are. Turn your grill to high and grill your bacon rashers for 5-7 minutes either side, or until crispy.

3. Transfer your oats to bowl and crumble over your crispy bacon. Serve with additional topping such as extra cheese, caramelised onions, wilted spinach, avocado, or a fried egg.

BREAKFAST CASSEROLE

SERVES	6
CALORIES	307
CARBOHYDRATES	30.3g
PROTEIN	18.5g
FAT	13.1g

INGREDIENTS

- 8 medium eggs
- 4 egg whites
- 180ml // ¾ c full fat milk
- 1 tsp Dijon mustard
- 1 garlic clove, minced
- 2 medium sweet potatoes, peeled and grated
- 1 small brown onion, sliced
- 1 red pepper, diced
- 1 small broccoli head, cut into florets
- 110g // ½ c cheddar cheese, grated
- Salt and Pepper to taste

DIRECTIONS

1. In a medium mixing bowl whisk together your eggs, egg whites, milk, mustard, and garlic. Season with salt and pepper and set aside.

2. Grease the bowl of your slow cooker before placing in your grated potatoes, onion, red pepper, and broccoli. Mix everything together before pouring over your egg mixture and mixing again.

3. Sprinkle over your grated cheese before setting your slow cooker to 'low' and leaving to cook for 4 hours. After 4 hours check that your eggs are cooked through and your potatoes are softened.

4. Serve immediately, garnished with fresh basil or chopped spring onion.

APRICOT AND ALMOND PORRIDGE

SERVES	6
CALORIES	485
CARBOHYDRATES	39.7g
PROTEIN	11.7g
FAT	34.2g

INGREDIENTS

- 500ml // 2 c almond milk
- 500ml // 2 c water (extra if necessary)
- 200g // 1 c oats
- ½ tsp almond extract
- 170g // ¾ c dried apricots, roughly chopped
- 2 tbsp apricot jam
- 140g // 1 c almonds, roughly chopped

DIRECTIONS

1. Pour your almond milk, water, oats, almond extract, and half your dried apricots into the bowl of your slow cooker and stir to mix. Set your slow cooker to 'low' and leave your oats to cook for 8 hours, preferably overnight.

2. Once cooked see if extra water is necessary to thin the oats. Stir in your remaining dried apricots, apricot jam, and chopped almonds, then set your slow cooker to 'high' in order to reheat your porridge.

3. Spoon your oats into serving bowls and serve topped with Greek yoghurt, fresh apricots, or more crushed almonds.

MAINS

MAINS

A selection of delicious dishes from all over the world, featuring a variety of meats, flavours, and slow cooking methods

PORK LOIN WITH BACON AND GARLIC

SERVES	8
CALORIES	546
CARBOHYDRATES	9.9g
PROTEIN	55.7g
FAT	30.4g

INGREDIENTS

- 1.4 kg // 3 lb. pork loin
- 1 tbsp olive oil
- 4 garlic cloves, minced
- 75g // 1/3 c golden caster sugar
- 8 rashers of back bacon
- Salt and Pepper to taste

DIRECTIONS

1. Prepare your pork by trimming off any excess fat. Massage your olive oil all over the loin, then season with salt and pepper and massage again.

2. Sprinkle your minced garlic and caster sugar along the top of the loin, spreading to coat all the top. Arrange your bacon rashers on top of the seasoned loin, tucking the edges under the bottom of the loin if your rashers are long enough.

3. Set your slow cooker to 'low' and roast your pork loin for 4-5 hours, or until cooked through and with crispy bacon. If you want to crisp your bacon further place it under a hot grill for a couple of minutes.

4. Serve your pork sliced, with sides of garlic mashed potatoes and seasonal veg.

SRIRACHA PULLED CHICKEN

SERVES	4
CALORIES	602
CARBOHYDRATES	22.4g
PROTEIN	43.6g
FAT	35.8g

INGREDIENTS

- 125ml // ½ c sriracha sauce
- 2 garlic cloves, minced
- 4 tbsp honey
- 2 tbsp fresh lime juice
- 1 tbsp lime zest
- 4 chicken breasts
- 1 yellow onion, thickly sliced

DIRECTIONS

1. Place your sriracha, minced garlic, honey, lime juice, and lime zest in a small mixing bowl. In a separate bowl place your chicken breast and sliced onions- pour over your sauce and toss together to ensure all the chicken is coated.

2. Transfer your coated chicken breasts to your slow cooker and cook on 'high' for 3-4 hours, or until the chicken is tender and cooked through. Once cooked remove your chicken from the slow cooker and shred using two forks.

3. Serve the chicken with rice and fresh vegetables, or mix with fresh coriander and use to fill tacos and enchiladas.

TERIYAKI PULLED PORK

SERVES	6
CALORIES	705
CARBOHYDRATES	4.8g
PROTEIN	55.1g
FAT	50g

INGREDIENTS

- 1.4 kg // 3 lb. pork shoulder
- 60ml // ¼ c dark soy sauce
- 2 tbsp dark brown muscovado sugar
- 1 tsp ground ginger
- 2 garlic cloves, minced
- 2 tsp garlic powder
- 1 tsp salt
- 1 tsp fresh black pepper
- 1 tsp chilli flakes
- 1 tbsp plain flour
- 125ml // ½ c water
- 60ml // ¼ c apple cider vinegar

DIRECTIONS

1. Prepare your pork should by removing as much fat as possible. Once the pork is prepared transfer it to the bowl of your slow cooker.

2. Place your soy sauce, sugar, ground ginger, minced garlic, garlic powder, salt, pepper, chilli, and flour in a small bowl, and mix everything together. Pour this over your pork and massage it in, ensure all of the pork is coated.

3. Pour your water and vinegar over the seasoned pork before setting your slow cooker to 'low' and leaving to cook for 8-10 hours. Cook your pork until is it tender and fragrant.

4. Once cooked remove your pork from the slow cooker and shred using 2 forks. Serve your pulled pork in bao buns with shredded vegetables, in tacos or burritos, or with rice and steamed vegetables.

SPICY BUTTERNUT SOUP

SERVES	6
CALORIES	166
CARBOHYDRATES	18.7g
PROTEIN	3g
FAT	10.3g

INGREDIENTS

- 1 large butternut squash, peeled, deseeded, and diced
- 1 yellow onion, diced
- 1 l // 4 c vegetable stock
- 1 can of coconut milk
- 3 tbsp Thai red curry paste
- 2 tsp chilli flakes

DIRECTIONS

1. Place your diced butternut, diced onion, and vegetable stock into your slow cooker. Set your slow cooker to 'high' and leave for 5 hours, or until the butternut is softened.

2. Once the butternut is cooked and softened use a handheld blender to puree the mixture. Pour in your can of coconut milk, curry paste, and chilli flakes, then blend again until everything is smooth, creamy, and combined.

3. Replace the lid and set your slow cooker to 'low' again, cooking the soup for another hour to infuse the flavour throughout. Once infused and heated serve immediately, topping with more chilli flakes and a fresh line wedge.

BEEF STEW

SERVES	8
CALORIES	344
CARBOHYDRATES	26.8g
PROTEIN	40.3g
FAT	7.5g

INGREDIENTS

- 900g // 2lb. diced beef
- 6 tbsp plain flour
- ½ tsp onion powder
- 1 tsp Italian herb seasoning
- Salt and Pepper to taste
- 1 yellow onion, roughly cut
- 4 medium potatoes, peeled and roughly cut
- 3 carrots, peeled and roughly cut
- 2 celery sticks, roughly cut 4 garlic cloves, minced
- 1 l // 4 c beef stock
- 4 tbsp tomato paste
- 60ml // ¼ c tinned tomatoes
- 2 tbsp marmite

- ◆ 1 tbsp Italian herb seasoning
- ◆ Salt and Pepper to taste
- ◆ 2 tbsp cornflour
- ◆ 3 tbsp water

DIRECTIONS

1. Begin by placing your beef, flour, onion powder, Italian herbs, and seasoning in a large bowl. Massage the seasoning into the beef before placing it into the bowl of your slow cooker.

2. Arrange your onion, potatoes, carrots, and celery around your seasoned beef. In a large pan heat your beef stock to a simmer, then add your tomato paste, tinned tomatoes, marmite, Italian herbs, and seasoning, and stir to combine.

3. Allow the stock to cool to lukewarm before pouring into the slow cooker, on top of your arranged ingredients. Set your slow cooker to 'low' and cook for 5-7 hours, on until your beef is tender and cooked through. Taste and add extra seasoning if necessary.

4. In a small bowl mix your cornflour and water until a paste forms. Pour into your stew, stir, and increase your slow cookers heat to 'high'. Cook for another 20-30 minutes to thicken the sauce.

5. Serve immediately with brown rice and seasonal vegetables.

HONEY LIME CHICKEN

SERVES	8
CALORIES	256
CARBOHYDRATES	9.7g
PROTEIN	31.8g
FAT	9.6g

INGREDIENTS

- 6 chicken breasts
- 1 tbsp butter
- 60ml // ¼ c honey
- 125 ml // ½ c lime juice
- 2 tsp chilli powder
- 1 tsp onion powder
- 2 garlic cloves, minced
- 1 tsp smoked paprika
- ½ tsp ground cumin
- 1 tsp salt
- 1 tsp cracked black pepper
- 250ml // 1 c salsa verde sauce

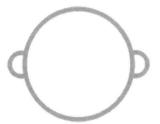

DIRECTIONS

1. Begin by melting your butter and brushing it all over your chicken breasts. In a small bowl mix together your honey, lime juice, chilli powder, onion powder, minced garlic, paprika, cumin, salt, and pepper. Rub this all over your chicken breasts, then place them in your slow cooker bowl.

2. Pour any of the remaining marinade into the bowl, then add your salsa verde sauce. Stir the mix to ensure the sauce covers all the chicken, then set your slow cooker to 'high'. Leave the chicken to cook for 2-4 hours, or until cooked through and tender.

3. Once cooked remove your chicken from the slow cooker and shred using 2 forks. Return the now shredded chicken to the slow cooker for a further 20 minutes.

4. Once 20 minutes has passed and the shredded chicken has absorbed as much sauce as possible remove it from the slow cooker to serve. Serve the chicken on flatbreads, in tacos, or in a spicy pasta sauce.

BUTTER CHICKEN CURRY

SERVES	4
CALORIES	505
CARBOHYDRATES	7.8g
PROTEIN	36.1g
FAT	36.5g

INGREDIENTS

CHICKEN
- 250ml // 1 c full fat plain yoghurt
- 1 tbsp lemon juice
- 1 tsp ground turmeric
- 2 tsp ground cumin
- 1 tsp cayenne pepper
- 1 tsp ground ginger
- 1 tsp cracked black pepper
- 1 tsp salt
- 3 chicken breasts, diced

SAUCE
- 1 tbsp butter
- 1 garlic clove, minced
- 1 chilli pepper, finely sliced

- ◆ 2 tsp ground cumin
- ◆ 2 tsp smoked paprika
- ◆ 1 can of tinned tomatoes
- ◆ 250ml // 1 c double cream
- ◆ 2 tbsp cornflour
- ◆ 1 tbsp water
- ◆ Salt and Pepper to taste
- ◆ 4 tbsp fresh coriander, chopped

DIRECTIONS

1. In a medium mixing bowl place your 'chicken' yoghurt, lemon juice, turmeric, cumin, cayenne pepper, ginger, black pepper, and salt. Mix everything together before adding in your diced chicken breasts. Stir thoroughly to ensure all the chicken is coated, then place in the fridge to marinate for at least 4 hours, preferably overnight.

2. Once the chicken has marinated sufficiently remove it from the fridge. Wipe off any excess marinade before placing the chicken into your slow cooker bowl. Add in the butter, garlic and chilli pepper, and mix together.

3. In a separate bowl place your 'sauce' cumin, smoked paprika, tinned tomatoes, and double cream. Season with salt and pepper before stirring to combine. Pour this sauce over your chicken before setting your slow cooker to 'low' and leaving to cook for 4-5 hours.

4. Just before your chicken is cooked entirely mix together your cornflour and water. Pour this into the chicken mixture and stir vigorously to combine. Replace the lid and cook on 'high' for another 20-30 minutes, or until the chicken is tender and cooked through.

5. Remove from the slow cooker and serve immediately. Top with your chopped coriander and any additional items, such as yoghurt, rice, naan, or vegetables.

MONGOLIAN STEAK STIR FRY

SERVES	6
CALORIES	458
CARBOHYDRATES	34g
PROTEIN	235.1g
FAT	20g

INGREDIENTS

- 680g // 1.5 lb. steak, cut into thick strips

- 4 tbsp cornflour

- 2 tbsp coconut oil, melted

- 2 garlic cloves, minced

- 180ml // ¾ c soy sauce

- 180ml // ¾ c water

- 60 ml // ¼ c lime juice

- 1 tsp cayenne pepper

- 1 tsp chilli flakes

- 175g // ¾ c dark brown muscovado sugar

- 2 medium carrots, peeled and grated

- ½ small broccoli head, cut into florets

DIRECTIONS

1. Place your steak strips into a large bowl and sprinkle over your cornflour. Toss everything together, ensuring all your steak is coated in cornflour.

2. Pour your coconut oil, garlic, soy sauce, water, lime juice, cayenne pepper, chilli flakes, sugar, and carrots into your slow cooker bowl, and stir to combine. Add in your coated steak strips and stir once again, being sure to coat all the steak with sauce.

3. Set your slow cooker to 'low' and cook the steak for 4-5 hours, or until cooked through and tender. When the steak is almost done stir in your broccoli florets. Replace the lid and cook for a further 10 minutes.

4. Remove for your slow cooker and serve immediately. Ladle over rice or noodles, and garnish with spring onions and other green vegetables.

MACARONI CHEESE

SERVES	8
CALORIES	552
CARBOHYDRATES	31g
PROTEIN	24.4g
FAT	36.8g

INGREDIENTS

- ♦ 300g // 2 c uncooked macaroni
- ♦ 4 tbsp salted butter
- ♦ 450g // 2 c cheddar cheese, grated
- ♦ 3 medium eggs
- ♦ 125ml // ½ c sour cream
- ♦ 125ml // ½ c double cream
- ♦ 125ml // ½ c full fat milk
- ♦ 1 tsp mustard
- ♦ 1 tsp mustard powder
- ♦ 200g // 1 c mozzarella cheese, grated
- ♦ Salt and Pepper to taste

DIRECTIONS

1. Bring a large pan of salted water to the boil, then add your dry macaroni and cook for 5-7 minutes, or until cooked but retaining some bite. Pour the cooked pasta into your slow cooker bowl.

2. In the same pan melt your butter and cheddar. Once melted remove from the heat and allow to cool for a couple of minutes before whisking in your eggs, sour cream, double cream, milk, mustard, and mustard powder. Season the sauce with salt and pepper, then pour the sauce over your pasta.

3. In the slow cooker bowl mix together your macaroni and sauce, ensuring all the pasta is coated. Set your slow cooker to 'low' and leave to cook for 1 hour 30 minutes, stirring every half hour.

4. After 1 hour 30 minutes sprinkle your grated mozzarella over the macaroni. Replace the lid and leave the cheese to melt for 20 mins. Once melted remove the macaroni form the slow cooker.

5. If you like your cheese crispy place the dish under a hot grill for 3-5 minutes, otherwise serve immediately.

AUBERGINE BAKE

SERVES	6
CALORIES	377
CARBOHYDRATES	48.2g
PROTEIN	23.6g
FAT	12.4g

INGREDIENTS

- 1.8kg // 4 lb. aubergine, cut into 1cm rounds

- 1 tbsp salt

- 4 medium eggs

- 60ml // ¼ c full fat milk

- 160g // 1 ½ c breadcrumbs

- 90g // 3 oz. parmesan cheese, grated

- 2 tsp Italian herb seasoning

- 2 tsp smoked paprika

- 1 l // 4 c tomato sauce

- 450g // 16 oz. mozzarella cheese, grated

- 4 tbsp fresh basil, chopped

DIRECTIONS

1. Lay your aubergine out on a large baking tray and sprinkle each side of a round with salt. Leave for 30 minutes before removing the salt by wiping each round with a paper towel.

2. In a small mixing bowl whisk together your eggs and milk. In a separate bowl mix together your breadcrumbs, parmesan, Italian herb seasoning, and paprika. Divide your tomato sauce between 4 and layer the bottom of your slow cooker bowl with one of these quarters.

3. Dip an aubergine round in the egg mixture, then in the breadcrumb mixture, and then place it on top of the sauce in your slow cooker. Repeat until you have a layer of breaded aubergine.

4. Pour over another quarter of your sauce and sprinkle over a third of your mozzarella. Repeat this process twice more, so you have 3 layers of breaded aubergine, sauce, and cheese.

5. Set your slow cooker to 'low' and bake your aubergine for 8 hours. After 7 hours and 30 minutes sprinkle over half of your fresh basil. Once 8 hours has passed remove your aubergine from the slow cooker, topping with the remaining fresh basil.

6. Serve immediately, as a side or tasty vegetarian main accompanied by crusty bread.

CAULIFLOWER CURRY

SERVES	6
CALORIES	335
CARBOHYDRATES	30.7g
PROTEIN	6.3g
FAT	23.1g

INGREDIENTS

- 1 large cauliflower head, cut into florets
- 1 red pepper, sliced
- 4 small potatoes, peeled and roughly chopped
- 1 yellow onion, diced
- 2 garlic cloves, minced
- 4 tbsp cashew nuts, crushed

SAUCE
- 500ml // 2 c vegetable stock
- 500ml // 2 c coconut milk
- 2 tbsp curry powder
- 1 tsp ground turmeric
- 1 tsp ground cumin
- 1 tsp cayenne pepper

DIRECTIONS

1. Place your cauliflower florets, red pepper, potatoes, onion, garlic, and 2 tbsp of crushed cashew nuts into your slow cooker. In a large saucepan heat your vegetable stock and half your coconut milk together, then add in curry powder, turmeric, cumin, and cayenne pepper. Leave simmering for 5 minutes before pouring into the slow cooker, over your arranged vegetables.

2. Stir everything to combine, ensuring all your vegetables are coated with some sauce. Set your slow cooker to 'low' and leave to cook for 4 hours. After 3 hours and 30 minutes pour in the rest of your coconut milk and stir to combine before covering and leaving for the remaining half hour.

3. Serve immediately, garnished with the remaining crushed cashew nuts. The curry goes perfectly with rice, zoodles, or naan breads.

CHICKEN AND MUSHROOM STROGANOFF

SERVES	4
CALORIES	557
CARBOHYDRATES	5.3g
PROTEIN	31.2g
FAT	46.2g

INGREDIENTS

- 4 chicken breasts, cut into bite sized chunks

- 225g // 8 oz. mushrooms, washed and destalked

- 225g // 8 oz. cream cheese, softened

- 250ml // 1 c chicken stock

- 250ml // 1 c double cream

- 2 tsp onion powder

- 2 bay leaves

- Salt and Pepper to taste

DIRECTIONS

1. Place your cut chicken into the bowl of your slow cooker. Cut your mushrooms, slicing some and dicing other in order to add extra texture to your dish. Once cut add these in with your chicken.

2. In a medium saucepan heat together your cream cheese, chicken stock, double cream, onion powder, and bay leaves. Once everything is combined season with salt and pepper and pour into your slow cooker bowl.

3. Set your slow cooker to 'low' and cook for 5 hours, or until the chicken is tender and cooked through. Stir every hour to ensure even cooking, but be careful not to break the bay leaves.

4. Once cooked remove from the slow cooker and fish out the bay leaves. Serve immediately, using the stroganoff to top egg noodles or rice, and garnishing with fresh parsley.

HONEYED PARMESAN PORK ROAST

SERVES	6
CALORIES	726
CARBOHYDRATES	24.5g
PROTEIN	67.7g
FAT	38.5g

INGREDIENTS

- 1.4kg // 3 lb. pork loin
- 60g // 2/3 c grated parmesan
- 125ml // ½ c honey
- 3 tbsp dark soy sauce
- 2 tbsp dried rosemary, chopped
- 1 tbsp dried basil
- 1 tbsp dried thyme
- 1 tbsp dried oregano
- 2 garlic cloves, minced
- 2 tbsp salted butter
- 2 tbsp cornflour
- 125ml // ½ c chicken stock

DIRECTIONS

1. Place your pork loin into the slow cooker bowl. In a small bowl mix together your parmesan, honey, soy sauce, rosemary, basil, thyme, oregano, garlic, and butter. Pour or brush this marinade over your pork, being sure to cover all the meat.

2. Leave your pork loin to stand for 20-30 minutes before setting your slow cooker to 'low' and roasting your pork for 5-6 hours, or until cooked through and tender. Once cooked remove from the slow cooker and leave to rest.

3. As the pork rests heat your chicken stock and any excess roasting juice in a small saucepan. Add the cornflour and whisk quickly until the sauce begins to thicken.

4. Once the sauce has thickened slice your pork. Serve warm, drizzled with sauce and accompanied by honeyed parsnips or other seasonal veg.

MOROCCAN BEEF STEW

SERVES	6
CALORIES	448
CARBOHYDRATES	43.8g
PROTEIN	42.4g
FAT	10.8g

INGREDIENTS

- 750g // 1.6 lb. beef, cut into chunks
- 1 tbsp fresh grated ginger
- 1 tsp ground ginger
- 2 tbsp ground cinnamon
- 1 tbsp ground cumin
- 2 tsp ground turmeric
- 1 tsp fresh black pepper
- 1 tsp coarse sea salt
- 1 brown onion, sliced
- 4 large sweet potatoes, peeled and roughly chopped
- 1 can of tinned tomatoes
- 125ml // ½ c beef stock
- 55g // 1/3 c raisin mix
- 75g // 1/3 c feta, crumbled

DIRECTIONS

1. Heat some oil in a large frying pan. Pour in your cut beef and quickly brown the meat by frying on a high heat for 3-5 minutes. Once browned transfer your beef to your slow cooker bowl.

2. Mix your fresh ginger, ground ginger, cinnamon, cumin, turmeric, pepper, and salt in a small bowl. Place your onion and sweet potatoes in the slow cooker bowl with your beef, then sprinkle over your seasoning. Toss everything together with a wooden spoon, ensuring all the beef and vegetables are coated and seasoned.

3. Pour in your tinned tomatoes and beef stock and mix once again. Set you slow cooker to 'low' and leave to cook for 5 hours and 30 minutes, stirring every hour to ensure even cooking.

4. Once tis time has passed stir for a final time before arranging your raisin mix and feta on top of the stew, the replacing the lid and leaving to cook for a further 30 minutes, or until the beef is cooked through and tender.

5. Serve immediately, accompanied by couscous or flatbread, and garnished with slivered almonds, lime wedges, and fresh coriander.

IRISH LAMB SHANKS

SERVES	4
CALORIES	467
CARBOHYDRATES	28.4g
PROTEIN	35.3g
FAT	19.4g

INGREDIENTS

- ♦ 4 lamb shanks
- ♦ 1 leek, thinly sliced
- ♦ 2 celery sticks, thinly sliced
- ♦ 3 carrots, peeled and diced
- ♦ 3 garlic cloves, minced
- ♦ 500ml // 2 c beef stock
- ♦ 250ml // 1 c of Irish stout beer, e.g. Guinness, Murphy's, or Beamish brands
- ♦ 2 tbsp tomato puree
- ♦ Salt and Pepper to taste
- ♦ 1 tbsp cornflour
- ♦ 1 tbsp water

DIRECTIONS

1. Prepare your lamb shanks by trimming off any excess fat. Heat some oil in a large pan and brown your lamb shanks, cooking on a high heat for 5-8 minutes and turning often. Once all shanks are browned transfer them to the bowl of your slow cooker.

2. In the same pan place your leek, celery, and carrot. Cook on a medium heat until softened, then add your garlic, season with salt and pepper, and cook for a further minute before mixing with your lamb shanks.

3. Mix together your beef stock, beer, and tomato puree. Pour this liquid over your lamb in the slow cooker, then set your slow cooker to 'low' and leave for 6 hours. Once tender and cooked through remove your lamb from the slow cooker.

4. Drain the liquid from the shanks. Heat the liquid in a medium saucepan over a high heat in order to reduce and thicken the mixture. Once the mixture has reached a simmer mix together your cornflour and water, then quickly whisk this into the sauce. Keep the sauce cooking until adequately thickened.

5. Serve your shanks warm, pouring over the sauce and accompanied by mashed potatoes and green beans or broccoli.

WILD EARTH MUSHROOM NOURISH BOWL

SERVES	6
CALORIES	537
CARBOHYDRATES	42.8g
PROTEIN	12.3g
FAT	33.7g

INGREDIENTS

- 200g // 1 c dry wild rice blend
- 1 yellow onion, diced
- 5 medium carrots, peeled and roughly chopped
- 1.25 l // 5 c vegetable stock
- 250ml // 1 c dry white wine
- 2 tbsp fresh thyme, finely chopped
- 1 bay leaf
- 50g // ½ c grated parmesan
- 250ml // 1 c double cream
- 1 tsp turmeric
- 1 tsp cayenne pepper
- 1 tsp smoked paprika

- 1 tsp cracked black pepper

- 4 garlic cloves, minced

- 8 tbsp salted butter, melted

- 900g // 2 lb. mushrooms-
  use a mix of different
  mushrooms and roughly tear
  for texture

- Salt and Pepper to taste

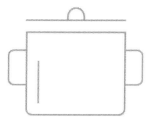

DIRECTIONS

1. Place your rice, onion, carrots, vegetable stock, wine, thyme, and bay leaf. Season with salt and pepper and roughly mix before setting your slow cooker to 'low' and leaving to cook for 6-8 hours.

2. After 6 hours remove the bay leaf and stir in your grated parmesan and cream. Cook until the rice has absorbed most of the liquid and retains just a little bit of bite. Turn off your slow cooker but leave the rice in the bowl with the lid in place.

3. Preheat your oven to 200C // 400F. In a large mixing bowl toss together your turmeric, cayenne pepper, paprika, black pepper, garlic, melted butter, and mushrooms. Be sure the mushrooms are fully coated before transferring to a large baking tray and roasting in your preheated oven for 40-50 minutes, stirring halfway.

4. Once golden and roasted pour the whole contents of the baking tray into your rice and stir to combine. Set your slow cooker to high in order to reheat your rice. Once adequately heated transfer to bowls and serve, garnishing with fresh thyme, parmesan, and any extra mushrooms.

CHEESE TORTELLINI

SERVES	4
CALORIES	552
CARBOHYDRATES	46.1g
PROTEIN	55.5g
FAT	15.4g

INGREDIENTS

- ◆ 450g // 1 lb. beef mince
- ◆ 1 brown onion, diced and sliced
- ◆ 3 garlic cloves, minced
- ◆ 2 cans of tinned tomatoes
- ◆ 1 green chilli, finely sliced
- ◆ 1 tsp dried basil
- ◆ 1 tsp dried oregano
- ◆ 1 tsp smoked paprika
- ◆ 250g // 9 oz. ready made cheese tortellini
- ◆ 225g // 1 c mozzarella cheese, grated
- ◆ 100g // ½ c cheddar cheese, grated

♦ 4 tbsp fresh basil, finely sliced

DIRECTIONS

1. Heat some olive oil in a large pan. Add in your beef mince, onion, and garlic, and cook for 3-5 minutes, or until the beef is split and browned. Remove from the heat, drain any excess fat, and then transfer to your slow cooker bowl.

2. Pour in your tinned tomatoes, green chilli, dried basil, dried oregano, and paprika. Stir to combine before setting your slow cooker to 'high' and leaving to cook for 3-4 hours.

3. Once the beef is cooked stir in your tortellini. Sprinkle over your grated mozzarella, grated cheddar, and fresh basil. Replace the lid and turn your slow cooker down to 'low'. Cook for another 20-30 minutes, or until the tortellini is cooked through and the cheese has all melted.

4. Serve immediately, garnished with extra basil and a sprinkle of chilli flakes.

PAELLA

SERVES	6
CALORIES	541
CARBOHYDRATES	37.6g
PROTEIN	48.2g
FAT	19.5g

INGREDIENTS

- ◆ 680g // 1.5 lb. chicken breast, cut into bite sized pieces

- ◆ 230g // 0.5 lb. chorizo, sliced and diced

- ◆ 200g // 1 c arborio rice

- ◆ 1 can of tinned tomatoes

- ◆ 1 yellow onion, sliced

- ◆ 4 garlic cloves, minced

- ◆ 1 tsp garlic powder

- ◆ 1 tsp onion powder

- ◆ 1 tbsp smoked paprika

- ◆ ½ tsp cayenne pepper

- ◆ 500ml // 2 c chicken stock

- ◆ 60ml // ¼ c dry white wine

- ◆ 60ml // ¼ c fresh lemon juice

- ◆ 230g // 0.5 lb. shrimp, peeled and deveined

- ◆ 150g // 1 c frozen peas

- ◆ Salt and Pepper to taste

DIRECTIONS

1. Heat some oil in a large pan. Add your chicken and chorizo and fry for 7-10 minutes, or until the chicken is golden and crisped. Transfer this mix to your slow cooker bowl.

2. Pour in your rice, tinned tomatoes, onion, garlic, garlic powder, onion powder, paprika, and cayenne pepper. Stir everything together before seasoning with salt and pepper, and pouring over your chicken stock, white wine, and lemon juice. Stir until everything is thoroughly combined.

3. Set your slow cooker to 'low' and cook for 1-2 hours, stirring every 30 minutes. Once the rice is cooked through but retaining a little bite add in your shrimp and frozen peas. Replace the lid and cook for another 10 minutes, or until the shrimp are pink and warm.

4. Serve the paella immediately, garnished with a lemon wedge and fresh parsley.

BEAN NON-CARNE

SERVES	4
CALORIES	344
CARBOHYDRATES	75.5g
PROTEIN	10.2g
FAT	1g

INGREDIENTS

- ◆ 3 cans tinned tomatoes
- ◆ 1 tbsp chilli powder
- ◆ 1 tbsp smoked paprika
- ◆ 1 tbsp ground cumin
- ◆ 1 tsp marmite
- ◆ 2 tsp dark brown muscovado sugar
- ◆ 2 garlic cloves, minced
- ◆ 1 can of kidney beans
- ◆ 1 can of 3 bean salad
- ◆ 1 can of black beans
- ◆ 3 medium sweet potatoes, peeled and roughly chopped
- ◆ 2 carrots, peeled and roughly chopped
- ◆ 1 brown onion, sliced

♦ Salt and Pepper to taste

DIRECTIONS

1. Pour your tinned tomatoes, chilli powder, paprika, cumin, marmite, sugar, and garlic into a large saucepan. Heat on medium for 10-15 minutes, stirring regularly, until fragrant and bubbling.

2. Whilst the sauce is on the heat pour the entire contents of your tinned beans into your slow cooker bowl. Add in your potatoes, carrots, and onion, and stir to mix everything together.

3. Pour over your heated sauce and season with salt and pepper. Set your slow cooker to 'low' and leave to cook for 7-8 hours. The chilli will be cooked once your potato and carrots are softened and the sauce has thickened.

4. Serve immediately, accompanied by brown rice or tortillas, and topped with sour cream and fresh coriander.

LASAGNE

SERVES	6
CALORIES	441
CARBOHYDRATES	33.5g
PROTEIN	47.2g
FAT	12.6g

INGREDIENTS

- ◆ 1 brown onion, sliced and diced
- ◆ 3 garlic cloves, minced
- ◆ 450g // 1 lb. beef mince
- ◆ 1 can of tinned tomatoes
- ◆ 3 tbsp tomato puree
- ◆ 1 tsp dried basil
- ◆ 1 tsp dried oregano
- ◆ 2 tsp Italian herb seasoning
- ◆ 1 packet of lasagne sheets
- ◆ 340g // 12 oz. cottage cheese
- ◆ 450g // 2 c grated mozzarella cheese
- ◆ 120g // ½ c grated cheddar cheese
- ◆ Salt and Pepper to taste

DIRECTIONS

1. Heat some oil in a large frying pan. Sautee your onion and garlic, and once softened add in your beef mince. Cook your beef mince for 5-7 minutes, or until browned and separated. Pour in your tinned tomatoes, tomato puree, oregano, basil, and Italian herb seasoning, then stir until everything is combined and heated.

2. In a separate bowl mix together your cottage cheese and mozzarella cheese. Season with salt and pepper.

3. Spoon a third of your beef mixture into your slow cooker bowl and top with a layer of lasagne sheets, before spreading over a third of your cheese mixture. Repeat this process twice more, so you are left with three layers of beef, pasta sheets, and cheese mixture.

4. Sprinkle your grated cheddar over the arranged lasagne. Set your slow cooker to 'low' and leave to cook for 4-6 hours. The lasagne will be ready once the cheese is melted, sauce is bubbling, and the lasagne sheets are soft.

5. Remove from the slow cooker and serve immediately, accompanied by garlic bread and a seasonal greens salad.

DESSERTS

DESSERTS

Cakes, bakes, and everything good that fills a plate- never go wrong with baking again using these tried and tested slow cooker dessert recipes

ALMOND AND ORANGE LOAF CAKE

SERVES	8
CALORIES	353
CARBOHYDRATES	43g
PROTEIN	5.5g
FAT	19.3g

INGREDIENTS

- ◆ 2 tbsp dark brown muscovado sugar

- ◆ 1 tbsp honey

- ◆ 2 oranges

- ◆ 125g // ½ c softened butter

- ◆ 170g // 6 oz. golden caster sugar

- ◆ 2 medium eggs

- ◆ 100g // ¾ c self-raising flour

- ◆ 85g // ¾ c ground almonds

DIRECTIONS

1. Start by lining a 8x4 inch loaf pan with parchment paper, leaving the paper long enough to hang over the sides of the pan. Mix together your muscovado sugar and honey in a small bowl and spread the mixture over the base of your pan.

2. Slice both of your oranges in half. Juice 3 of the halves, and thinly slice the remaining half, arranging the slices on top honey and sugar lined base.

3. Pour you butter and caster sugar into a medium mixing bowl and cream together using an electric whisk. Add your eggs, one at a time, checking that the mixture doesn't curdle as the eggs are added.

4. When the mixture is smooth and combined sift over your flour and ground almonds, then fold them into the mix- be gentle to prevent knocking any air from the creamed mix. Stir in half of your fresh orange juice.

5. Pour the mixture into your prepared pan and smooth the top. Place the pan into the bowl of your slow cooker, cover, and turn on 'high' to cook. Cook for 2 hours and 30 minutes.

6. Once cooked turn off your slow cooker and leave the loaf cake to sit for 5 to 10 minutes. Remove from the slow cooker and turn onto a plate before brushing over the remaining orange juice.

7. Serve the cake warm with fresh cream and berries.

COFFEE CAKE

SERVES	8
CALORIES	449
CARBOHYDRATES	68.8g
PROTEIN	7.2g
FAT	16.7g

INGREDIENTS

- 310g // 2 ½ c plain flour
- 300g // 1 ½ c dark brown sugar
- 2 tsp baking powder
- 2 tsp cinnamon
- 140g // 2/3 c salted butter
- 1 tbsp coffee granules, mixed with 1 tbsp water
- 2 eggs
- 375ml // 1½ c milk

DIRECTIONS

1. Start by lining your slow cooker bowl or a 9x13" pan with greaseproof paper, or greasing with a thin layer of butter, or a non-stick alternative.

2. Sift your flour, sugar, baking powder, and cinnamon into a large mixing bowl. Add your butter and beat with a handheld whisk until the mixture has a crumbly texture like that of breadcrumbs. Pour in your dissolved coffee granules, eggs, and butter, and whisk again until a smooth batter forms.

3. Pour your batter into the prepared bowl and smooth the mixture down with a spatula or wooden spoon. Set your slow cooker to 'high' and cook for 1 ½ - 2 ½ hours, checking readiness at each half hour by seeing whether an inserted skewer comes out clean.

4. Serve the cake warm with vanilla ice cream and a sprinkle of chopped walnuts.

CARROT CAKE WITH CREAM CHEESE FROSTING

SERVES	8
CALORIES	877
CARBOHYDRATES	142.2g
PROTEIN	9g
FAT	32.9g

INGREDIENTS

♦ 280g // 1 ¼ c applesauce

♦ 400g // 2 c light brown sugar

♦ 3 medium eggs

♦ ½ tsp vanilla bean paste

♦ 250g // 2 c plain flour

♦ 1 tbsp baking powder

♦ 1 tsp ground nutmeg

♦ 1 tsp ground allspice

♦ 1 tsp ground ginger

♦ 2 tsp ground cinnamon

♦ 2 medium carrots, peeled and grated

♦ 100g // 1 c desiccated coconut

- 125ml // ½ c pineapple, apple, or orange juice

FROSTING
- 120g // ½ c butter, softened

- 240 g // 8 oz. cream cheese, softened

- ½ tsp salt

- ½ tsp vanilla bean paste

- 450g // 1 lb icing sugar

DIRECTIONS

1. Start by lining the bowl of your slow cooker or a circular cake pan with greaseproof paper, leaving the paper long enough to hang over the sides of the pan.

2. Place your applesauce, sugar, eggs, and vanilla bean paste in a large mixing bowl, and beat together using a handheld whisk. Sift in your flour, baking powder, nutmeg, allspice, ginger, and cinnamon, then beat with the handheld whisk once again until just combined.

3. Add your carrots, desiccated coconut, and juice to the batter. Take a wooden spoon and mix in these ingredients until just combined, then pour the batter into your prepared pan.

4. Set your slow cooker to 'low' and bake your cake for 3 hours. Times will vary depending upon your slow cooker, so check every 15-30 minutes once the cake has been baking for 2 hours and 30 minutes- this will also release some excess steam that may otherwise affect your cake.

5. Once a skewer is inserted and comes out clean, then your cake is baked through. Remove it from the slow cooker and set aside to cool completely before removing from the pan.

6. As the cake cools make your cream cheese frosting. Place your butter, cream cheese salt, vanilla bean paste, and icing sugar in a medium mixing bowl, and beat on a high speed using a handheld whisk. When the icing is white and fluffy it is ready.

7. Assemble your cake by cutting the cooled cake in half. Divide your frosting in two, using one half to fill the cake and the other half to spread on top. Decorate your cake as desired, topping with more desiccated coconut, crushed nuts, or fruit peel.

STICKY CARAMEL CAKE

SERVES	8
CALORIES	548
CARBOHYDRATES	98.6g
PROTEIN	7.5g
FAT	15.5g

INGREDIENTS

- ◆ 325g // 2 ½ c plain flour
- ◆ 400 g // 2 c golden caster sugar
- ◆ 4 tbsp dark brown muscovado sugar
- ◆ 3 tsp baking powder
- ◆ 125g // ½ c salted butter, softened
- ◆ 3 medium eggs
- ◆ 60ml // ¼ c boiling water
- ◆ 125ml // ½ c caramel sauce or dulce de leche

DIRECTIONS

1. Start by lining the bowl of your slow cooker or a large circular cake pan with greaseproof paper, leaving the paper long enough to hang over the sides of the pan.

2. Place your flour, caster sugar, muscovado sugar, and baking powder in a large mixing bowl and mix together using a handheld whisk. Beat in your butter, then crack in your eggs one at a time, beating the mixture in between adding each egg to avoid curdling.

3. Pour the batter into your prepared pan and smooth the surface. In a small bowl or jug mix together your caramel sauce and boiling water, then drizzle this over your batter.

4. Set your slow cooker to 'high' and bake your cake for 2 hours. Times will vary depending upon your slow cooker, so check every 15-20 minutes once the cake has been baking for 1 hours and 30 minutes- this will also release some excess steam that may otherwise affect your cake.

5. Remove your cake from the slow cooker once is it done. This is a sticky cake, so you may test it with a skewer, but it is likely caramel or crumbs will stick to the skewer and this may give the false impression it isn't ready.

6. Serve the cake warm with praline, vanilla ice cream, and a drizzling of caramel sauce.

GERMAN CHOCOLATE CAKE

SERVES	8
CALORIES	456
CARBOHYDRATES	77.8g
PROTEIN	7.1g
FAT	16.3g

INGREDIENTS

- ◆ 2 medium eggs
- ◆ 125g // ½ c salted butter
- ◆ 250 ml // 1 c full-fat milk
- ◆ 1 tbsp vanilla extract
- ◆ 400g // 2 c caster sugar
- ◆ 220g // 1 ¾ c plain flour
- ◆ 75g // ¾ c cocoa powder
- ◆ 1 tbsp baking powder
- ◆ 250ml // 1 c boiling water

DIRECTIONS

1. Start by lining the bowl of your slow cooker or a circular cake pan with greaseproof paper, leaving the paper long enough to hang over the sides of the pan.

2. Place your eggs, butter, milk, and vanilla extract into a medium mixing bowl and whisk using a handheld whisk. Pour in your caster sugar, flour, cocoa powder, and baking powder, then whisk again to combine.

3. Keeping your whisk on, pour in your boiling water in a thin stream. You may not need all the water, so once your batter is wet and sticky, but you would not be able to pour it easily, stop.

4. Pour your batter into your prepared pan and place in your slow cooker on the 'low' setting. Bake for 3 hours. Times will vary depending upon your slow cooker, so check every 15-30 minutes once the cake has been baking for 2 hours and 30 minutes.

5. Once your cake is cooked through turn off your slow cooker and leave your cake to cool, leaving the lid slightly angled to allow the heat to escape. Serve your cake warm or cold with fresh berries, cream, and chocolate sauce.

GINGERBREAD CAKE

SERVES	8
CALORIES	287
CARBOHYDRATES	40.7g
PROTEIN	2.9g
FAT	13.1g

INGREDIENTS

CAKE

- 60g // ¼ c butter, softened

- 50g // ¼ c golden caster sugar

- 1 large egg

- ½ tsp vanilla bean extract

- 140g // ¼ c molasses

- 250ml // 1 c water

- 150g // 1 ¼ c plain flour

- 1 tsp bicarbonate of soda

- ½ tsp ground nutmeg

- ½ tsp ground cinnamon

- 1 tsp ground ginger

SAUCE

- ◆ 6 tbsp dark brown muscovado sugar

- ◆ 125ml // ½ c boiling water

- ◆ 2 tbsp lemon juice

- ◆ 60g // ¼ c butter

DIRECTIONS

1. Start by lining the bowl of your slow cooker or a circular cake pan with greaseproof paper, leaving the paper long enough to hang over the sides of the pan.

2. In a medium mixing bowl use a handheld whisk and cream together 'cake' butter and sugar. Once creamed crack in your egg and vanilla bean extract, and beat until just combined. Slowly pour in your molasses and water, beating on low until just combined.

3. Sift over your flour, bicarbonate of soda, nutmeg, cinnamon, and ginger. Gently fold these into your wet mixture, being careful to keep in as much air as is possible. Pour your batter into the prepared baking pan and smooth the top.

4. Sprinkle your 'sauce' dark brown sugar over the batter. Combine your boiling water, lemon juice, and butter in a mixing jug and pour this over your batter also. Transfer to your slow cooker and bake on 'high' for 2-3 hours. After 2 hours check if your cake is cooked by inserting a skewer. Leave baking until the skewer comes out clean.

5. Once baked remove the cake from your slow cooker. Serve immediately with vanilla ice cream or custard.

PLAIN CHEESECAKE

SERVES	12
CALORIES	466
CARBOHYDRATES	32.6g
PROTEIN	8.8g
FAT	34.5g

INGREDIENTS

BASE

- ◆ 150g // 1 ½ c digestive biscuits, crushed

- ◆ 4 tbsp butter, melted

- ◆ ½ tsp salt

FILLING

- ◆ 700g // 24 oz. cream cheese, softened

- ◆ 375ml // 1 ½ c sour cream

- ◆ 250g // 1 ¼ c golden caster sugar

- ◆ 5 large eggs

- ◆ 3 tbsp plain flour

- ◆ 2 tsp vanilla bean paste

DIRECTIONS

1. Start by lining the bowl of your slow cooker or a circular cake pan with greaseproof paper, leaving the paper long enough to hang over the sides of the pan. Set your slow cooker on 'low' to heat up.

2. Place your crushed biscuits, salt, and melted butter into a small bowl and mix to combine. Pour this base mixture into your pan and press down to create a smooth, even layer.

3. Place your cream cheese, sour cream, and caster sugar into a large mixing bowl. Use a handheld whisk on a high speed to beat them together. Add your eggs to the mix, cracking in one at a time and whisking until it is fully combined before adding the next. Sprinkle over your flour and vanilla bean paste, then whisk to combine for a final time.

4. Pour your cream cheese mixture over your prepared crust, smoothing the top and ensuring all sides or corners are filled. Place into your heating slow cooker and bake for 5-7 hours. Check every 30 minutes from 5 hours onwards to see if the cake is baked- it will be ready once an inserted skewer comes out clean.

5. Once baked remove your pan from the slow cooker and place the pan in the fridge. Allow the cake to set for at least 3 hours before removing from the pan and serving. This is just a basic plain cheesecake, so serve with whatever your heart may desire!

LAVENDER CRÈME BRULEE

SERVES	6
CALORIES	499
CARBOHYDRATES	24.8g
PROTEIN	4.9g
FAT	43.6g

INGREDIENTS

- ♦ 625ml // 2 ½ cups double cream

- ♦ 3 fresh sprigs of lavender, washed

- ♦ 1 tsp vanilla bean paste

- ♦ 6 large eggs, yolks and whites separated (the egg whites are not needed for this recipe)

- ♦ 110g // ½ c golden caster sugar

- ♦ 2 tbsp brown sugar

DIRECTIONS

1. Place your cream, lavender sprigs, and vanilla bean paste in a small saucepan. Bring the mixture to the boil, then immediately reduce the heat and leave the cream on a simmer.

2. In a clean glass mixing bowl place your egg yolks and caster sugar. Use a handheld whisk to beat them together, creating a creamy paste. Take your cream off the heat and remove the lavender sprigs.

3. Slowly pour your hot cream into your egg mix, whisking by hand as you do so. Only add the cream in a thin stream, ensuring it combines as you pour.

4. Divide the custard mixture between 6 ramekins. Arrange the ramekins in the bowl of your slow cooker, then pour boiling water into the bowl so it comes halfway up the ramekins.

5. Place the lid on your slow cooker and set to 'low', baking your custards for 2 hours, or until set with a wobble in the centre of the custard.

6. Once the custards are cooked remove them from the slow cooker and place them to chill in the fridge for at least 4 hours.

7. Just before serving remove your custards from the fridge and sprinkle with some brown sugar. Use a blow torch or a hot grill to melt and caramelise the sugar. Serve immediately, topped with a sprig of fresh lavender.

APPLE AND CHERRY CRUMBLE

SERVES	8
CALORIES	434
CARBOHYDRATES	79.1g
PROTEIN	3g
FAT	13.3g

INGREDIENTS

FILLING

- 3 tins of cherries, drained or 1 lb fresh cherries, pitted

- 3 large apples, peeled, cored, and cut into chunks

- 150g // 2/3 c golden caster sugar

- 4 tbsp plain flour

- Zest of 1 lemon

- 2 tbsp fresh lemon juice

- 2 tbsp apple juice

CRUMBLE

- 90g // 1 c rolled oats

- 100g // ½ c dark brown muscovado sugar

- 4 tbsp plain flour

- ◆ ½ tsp ground allspice
- ◆ ½ tsp ground nutmeg
- ◆ ½ tsp ground ginger
- ◆ 1 tsp ground cinnamon
- ◆ 120g // ½ c butter, cubed and cold

DIRECTIONS

1. Place your 'filling' cherries, apples, sugar, flour, and lemon zest in the bowl of your slow cooker and toss everything together so all the fruit is coated. Add your lemon and apple juice, then toss together once again.

2. Place your 'crumble' oats, sugar, flour, and spice in a medium mixing bowl or food processor. Stir or pulse the ingredients together, then add you cold butter and repeat to create a lumpy, sandy texture. If not using a food processor use your hands to rub the butter into your dry ingredients until a crumble has formed.

3. Pour your crumble over your fruit filling and set your slow cooker to 'high'. Leave your crumble to cook for 4 hours, opening the top every hour to release steam from the fruit filling. Once your crumble is golden and crisp remove from your slow cooker.

4. Serve warm with fresh custard, cream, or ice cream.

APPLE AND WALNUT BREAD PUDDING

SERVES	8
CALORIES	553
CARBOHYDRATES	90.5g
PROTEIN	13.6g
FAT	16.7g

INGREDIENTS

- ♦ 2 tbsp golden caster sugar

- ♦ 4 tbsp ground cinnamon

- ♦ 1 tsp ground nutmeg

- ♦ 2 tbsp lemon juice

- ♦ 3 large cooking apples, peeled, cored, ad cut into chunks

- ♦ 4 medium eggs

- ♦ 125ml // ½ c double cream

- ♦ 125ml // ½ c applesauce

- ♦ 125ml // ½ c caramel sauce or dulce de leche

- ♦ ½ tsp vanilla bean paste

- ♦ 100g // ½ c dark brown muscovado sugar

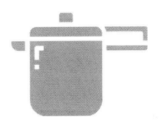

◆ 1 loaf of bread, stale and cut into 2x2cm cubes

◆ 60g // ½ c walnuts, chopped

DIRECTIONS

1. Start by lining the bowl of your slow cooker or a baking dish with greaseproof paper, leaving the paper long enough to hang over the sides of the pan.

2. Place your caster sugar, cinnamon, nutmeg, lemon juice, and apples in a bowl. Toss everything together to coat the apples, then set aside.

3. Pour your eggs, double cream, applesauce, caramel sauce, and vanilla bean paste into a large mixing bowl, and mix together using a handheld whisk until the mixture is creamy and foamy. Sprinkle over your muscovado sugar and whisk again until combined.

4. Assemble your bread pudding by arranging half of your cubed bread in your slow cooker bowl or baking dish. Sprinkle over half your coated apples, and half of your chopped walnuts, then pour over half of your beaten egg mixture. Repeat the process on top with the remaining half of your ingredients.

5. Shake your dish to spread the egg mixture before placing it into your slow cooker and setting the heat to 'low'. Bake for 3-4 hours, or until an inserted skewer comes out clean and the top is crispy and starting to brown. Turn off the heat and remove the lid of your slow cooker, then leave your bread pudding to set for 10 minutes.

6. After 10 minutes remove your bread pudding from the slow cooker and serve. Serve the pudding warm, topped with more chopped almonds and caramel sauce.

PEANUT BUTTER BROWNIES

SERVES	12
CALORIES	316
CARBOHYDRATES	39.5g
PROTEIN	5.7g
FAT	17.1g

INGREDIENTS

- 120g // ½ c salted butter, softened

- 75g // ¾ c cocoa powder

- 250g // 1 ¼ c light brown sugar

- ½ tsp salt

- 2 medium eggs

- 100g // 3/4 c plain flour

- 160g // 1 c chocolate chips

- 80g // 1/3 c crunchy peanut butter, melted

DIRECTIONS

1. Start by lining the bowl of your slow cooker or a baking dish with greaseproof paper, leaving the paper long enough to hang over the sides of the pan.

2. Place your butter, cocoa powder, sugar, salt, and eggs in a medium mixing bowl, and beat with a handheld whisk until smooth and creamy. Sift over your flour and gently fold into the mixture with a wooden spoon or spatula.

3. Sprinkle over half of your chocolate chips and gently stir to distribute throughout the mix. Pour you batter into your prepared dish before drizzling with your melted peanut butter and sprinkling over the remaining chocolate chips.

4. Bake your brownies on 'low' for 2 hours, then remove the lid from your slow cooker and bake for a further 20-30 minutes, depending on how gooey you like your brownies.

5. Once baked remove the brownies from the slow cooker and set aside to cool for 30-45 minutes. Cut your brownies into squares, and serve warmed slightly, or as they are.

CARAMEL BLONDIES

SERVES	12
CALORIES	138
CARBOHYDRATES	24.5g
PROTEIN	1.1g
FAT	4.2g

INGREDIENTS

- 200g // 1c dark brown muscovado sugar
- 60g // ¼ c salted butter
- 1 tsp vanilla bean paste
- 125g // 1 c plain flour
- 1 tsp baking powder
- 80ml // 1/3 c double cream
- 12 soft caramels, roughly cut
- 250ml // 1 c boiling water

DIRECTIONS

1. Start by lining the bowl of your slow cooker or a baking dish with greaseproof paper, leaving the paper long enough to hang over the sides of the pan.

2. In a medium mixing bowl cream half of your sugar with your butter, and vanilla bean paste using a handheld whisk. In a separate bowl sift together your flour and baking powder.

3. Taking a wooden spoon, stir half of your flour into your butter mix, then stir in half of your double cream. Repeat this with the remaining flour and cream. Once everything is combined sprinkle over your cut caramels and stir to distribute them throughout your batter. Pour the batter into your prepared dish and smooth the top.

4. In a small bowl dissolve your remaining sugar in your boiling water, stirring until no sugar granules are left. Pour this over your batter and place in your slow cooker to bake on 'high' for 2- 3 hours. Times will vary depending upon your slow cooker, so check every 15-30 minutes once the blondies have been baking for 2 hours.

5. Once an inserted skewer comes out clean and your blondies are cooked remove them from the slow cooker. Allow them to cool slightly before cutting, then serve with a drizzle of caramel sauce and whipped cream.

STRAWBERRY AND BASIL RICE PUDDING

SERVES	6
CALORIES	605
CARBOHYDRATES	115.8g
PROTEIN	14.5g
FAT	10.4g

INGREDIENTS

- 400g // 2 c uncooked white rice

- 700ml // 24 oz. evaporated milk

- 420ml // 14 oz. milk

- 300g // 1 ½ c golden caster sugar

- 150g // 1 c strawberries, washed and cut

- 4 tbsp fresh basil, finely sliced

DIRECTIONS

1. Place your rice, evaporated milk, milk, and caster sugar into the bowl of your slow cooker and stir to roughly combine. Sprinkle over half your strawberries and 3 tbsp of sliced basil.

2. Set your slow cooker to 'high' and cook for 3 hours, or until all the liquid is absorbed and the mix is thick and creamy. Stir halfway through cooking to ensure everything cooks evenly.

3. Once cooked sprinkle over your remaining strawberries and basil. Turn off your slow cooker and remove the lid, leaving your rice pudding to set for 15-20 minutes.

4. After 15-20 minutes remove your rice pudding from the slow cooker. Serve warm, topped with extra fruit or a sprig of basil.

STRAWBERRY AND BASIL RICE PUDDING

FUSS FREE FUDGE

SERVES	16
CALORIES	155
CARBOHYDRATES	22.3g
PROTEIN	1.7g
FAT	8.3g

INGREDIENTS

- 320g // 2 c dark chocolate chips

- 60ml // ¼ c double cream

- 80ml // 1/3 c honey

- 80g // ½ c white chocolate chips

- 1 tsp vanilla bean paste

- 2 tsp coarse sea salt

- 2 tbsp freeze dried raspberries

DIRECTIONS

1. Start by lining the bowl of your slow cooker or a baking dish with greaseproof paper, leaving the paper long enough to hang over the sides of the pan.

2. Add your dark chocolate chips, double cream, and honey to your prepared pan. Set your slow cooker on 'high' and cook for 1 hour. After one hour add your white chocolate chips and vanilla bean paste. Stir to combine, then cover for 10 minutes before stirring again.

3. Once your white chocolate is melted and combined remove your fudge mix from the slow cooker. Sprinkle over your sea salt and dried raspberries, then place in the fridge for 1-3 hours to cool.

4. Once cooled and firm cut your fudge into squares. Serve with fresh raspberries and vanilla ice cream.

COOKIES AND CREAM FUDGE

SERVES	36
CALORIES	113
CARBOHYDRATES	14g
PROTEIN	1g
FAT	5g

INGREDIENTS

- 400g // 2 ½ c white chocolate chips

- 1 tin of condensed milk

- 2 tsp vanilla bean paste

- 150g // 1 ½ c chocolate chip cookies

DIRECTIONS

1. Start by lining the bowl of your slow cooker or a baking dish with greaseproof paper, leaving the paper long enough to hang over the sides of the pan.

2. Place your white chocolate chips, condensed milk, and vanilla bean paste into your prepared pan, and stir a little to roughly distribute the chocolate. Transfer to your slow cooker and cook on 'low' for 30-40 minutes, stirring every 10 minutes.

3. Once the chocolate is all melted and everything is combined remove your fudge from the slow cooker. Ensure the top is smooth, the crumble over your chocolate chip cookies. If you wish, take a skewer and swirl your fudge to mix in some of the crumbled cookies.

4. Transfer to the fridge to cool for 2-4 hours. Once cooled and firmed cut into squares. Serve with more crumbled cookies and vanilla ice cream.

CHILLI HOT CHOCOLATE

SERVES	8
CALORIES	337
CARBOHYDRATES	19g
PROTEIN	6g
FAT	30g

INGREDIENTS

♦ 1 l // 4 c full fat milk

♦ 250ml // 1 c double cream

♦ 200g // 1 ½ c dark chocolate chips

♦ 100g // 2/3 c milk chocolate chips

♦ 1 tbsp ground cinnamon

♦ 1 tsp vanilla bean paste

♦ 2 red chilli peppers, halved and deseeded

♦ 1 tbsp light brown sugar

DIRECTIONS

1. Pour your milk, cream, and chocolate chips into your slow cooker and sir a little to ensure the milk and cream are combined. Cover and cook on 'low' for 1 hour, stirring after 30 minutes to ensure everything melts evenly.

2. After 1 hour add your ground cinnamon, vanilla bean paste, chilli peppers, and sugar. Leave heating in the slow cooker for another hour, once again stirring after 30 minutes.

3. Once everything is melted, heated, and infused to your liking remove the 4 chilli halves. Serve your hot chocolate with toasted marshmallows, whipped cream, and a grating of chocolate.

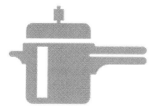

Printed in Great Britain
by Amazon